Active
Bulletin Boards

by
Wendy Everett

Illustrated by Dan Nevins

SCHOLASTIC INC.

NEW YORK · TORONTO · LONDON · AUCKLAND · SYDNEY · TOKYO

ISBN 0-590-31799-7

12 11 10 9 8 7 6 5 4 3 2   4 5 6 7 8 9/8

Printed in the U.S.A.   07

To a very special teacher,
Mary Everett

NOTE TO TEACHERS:

Have you ever looked at your classroom overflowing with 40 desks and wished you had the space to set up activity tables? Have you ever looked at your month-old bulletin boards and wondered what in the world you would put up next? If your answer is a resounding "*Yes!*", then "ACTIVE BULLETIN BOARDS" was written for you.

ACTIVE BULLETIN BOARDS is based on the concept that your bulletin boards are gold mines for keeping your students creatively productive when they have finished their assigned work. You don't have to squeeze tables into your classroom to give your students a special project to work on, or a learning game to enjoy. The ideas in this book will enable you to transform those sometimes intimidating spaces of cork into activity stations that will draw your students like magnets to stimulating and enjoyable learning challenges.

Some of the bulletin board ideas in this book are games that several students can play together. Some are activities which can be completed by one student alone. Others can be enjoyed by the entire class. All of the bulletin boards can be adjusted to fit specific grade-level requirements and particular classroom studies. Most importantly, all of them can be made with readily available school supplies, such as construction paper, tag board, crayons, pushpins, acetate sheets and grease pencils. *And,* much of the actual construction of the bulletin boards can be done by the students themselves!

CONTENTS

LANGUAGE ARTS

MATH

SCIENCE

SOCIAL STUDIES

SPEAK SPELLING WORDS

Purpose: Students practice their spelling words by writing them in complete sentences.

Materials:

1. Opaque projector
2. White paper to cover the board
3. Acetate sheets
4. Pictures of cartoon characters
5. Tag board
6. Grease pencils
7. Crayons
8. Felt-tipped marker
9. Construction paper

Making the Board:

1. Cover the board with white paper. Cut the words "SPEAK SPELLING WORDS" out of construction paper and staple them to the top of the board.

2. Use the opaque projector to draw two of your students' favorite cartoon characters onto the board. Allow the students to decorate the characters and background with crayons.

3. Cut two cartoon dialogue balloons out of tag board and cover them with acetate sheets or laminate them. Staple them to the board.

4. Make a score card and cover it with an acetate sheet or laminate it. Staple it to the board.

5. Make a spelling word check list and staple it to the board.

Using the Board:

Students write conversations between the two cartoon characters using as many spelling words in one sentence as possible. The sentences are written with grease pencil on the cartoon balloons and then the correct spelling is checked using the spelling check list.

Each student scores one point for every correctly spelled word that is used in a complete sentence. Words may be reused and prefixes and suffixes may be added. The next student to use the board erases the dialogue with a tissue. The conversations can continue indefinitely, or until a set number of points is reached.

This is a silent bulletin board activity, since everything the students have to say to each other can be written in the cartoon balloons.

STORY MAP

Purpose: Students develop their creative dramatic skills by re-enacting scenes from a well-known story and by creating new scenes based on the story.

Materials:

1. White paper to cover the board
2. Colored felt-tipped markers
3. Construction paper
4. Large cardboard box
5. Tag board
6. Plastic drinking straws
7. Crayons

Making the Board:

1. Cover the board with white paper. Cut the words for the story heading out of construction paper and staple them to the top of the board.

2. With a pencil, draw the places in the story where the important action takes place. Let the students embellish your drawing and color it with markers and crayons.

3. Have a group of students use the tag board to make "puppets" representing the characters of the story. Tape students' drawings of the characters to straws so that they can be handled easily. Staple the box to the board and place the puppets in it.

Using the Board:

Give students time to practice their own versions of scenes from the story and then let them perform for the entire class. This bulletin board idea can be used with just about any book. If you read to your class, use a book you have just finished, or let the class vote on their favorite story.

SILLY SENTENCES

Purpose: Students practice making complete sentences and review their knowledge of four parts of speech: nouns, adjectives, verbs, and adverbs.

Materials:

1. Construction paper
2. Tag board
3. Map pins
4. Three cardboard boxes
5. Felt-tipped marker
6. Paper hole punch
7. Decorative tape or masking tape

Making the Board:

1. Divide the board into four columns and as many horizontal rows as possible with strips of tape. (Leave space at the top of the board for the heading.)

2. Cut the words "SILLY SENTENCES" out of construction paper and staple them to the top of the board. Cut the words ADJECTIVE, NOUN, VERB, and ADVERB out of construction paper and staple them in that order at the top of each column.

3. Cut rectangles out of tag board and label them with different adjectives, nouns, verbs, and adverbs. (So that the words will form complete sentences more readily, make all the nouns plural.) Punch a hole in the top center of each card for hanging.

4. Push map pins into the board at the top center of each rectangular division.

5. Staple the three boxes to the board and place the word cards in them.

Using the Board:

Students will hang the word cards on the map pins in the proper columns. If the cards are not in the proper columns, the sentence will not make sense. If desired, the part of speech can be written on the back of the card to help the student check his or her work. After students become familiar with this activity, however, this shouldn't be necessary.

Allow the students to contribute cards of their own. Encourage them to choose words with some color so that the sentences will be more fun to make. You may want to include a few cards that don't fit into any of the categories, such as prepositions or conjunctions. When the students discover these "wild cards," these parts of speech can be discussed with the class.

WHICH GOES WHERE?

Purpose: Students review their knowledge of synonyms, antonyms, and homonyms.

Materials:

1. Construction paper
2. Tag board
3. Two cardboard boxes
4. Map pins
5. Felt-tipped marker
6. Paper hole punch
7. Acetate sheet
8. Grease pencil
9. Stop watch

Making the Board:

1. Cut the words "WHICH GOES WHERE?" out of construction paper and staple them to the top of the board. Cut the words SYNONYM, ANTONYM, and HOMONYM out of construction paper in another color and staple them to the board in three columns.

2. Cut long rectangles out of tag board. Label these with synonym pairs, antonym pairs, and homonym pairs. Punch a hole in the center of each card.

3. Place the map pins in the board so that the cards can be hung on them in three columns.

4. Staple the boxes to the board and place the tag board cards in them.

5. Make a time sheet with a space for the students' names and their times. Cover this with an acetate sheet or laminate it and staple it to the board.

Using the Board:

Students place the word pair cards in the appropriate columns. If they wish, they can time themselves with a stop watch and mark their best time on the time card with a grease pencil.

The cards can either be placed back in the boxes when the student is finished, or can be mixed up by the student, so that the next student has to unscramble them.

Keep changing the word pairs so that the activity is a constant challenge. Encourage the students to contribute their own word pair cards.

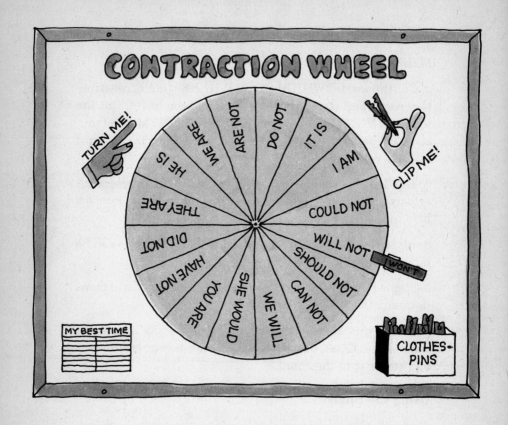

CONTRACTION WHEEL

Purpose: Students review their knowledge of contractions.

Materials:

1. Tag board
2. Clothespins (spring-clamp type)
3. Felt-tipped marker
4. Construction paper
5. Acetate sheet
6. Small cardboard box
7. Small nail or long-tined push pin
8. Grease pencil
9. Stop watch

Making the Board:

1. Cut the words "CONTRACTION WHEEL" out of construction paper and staple them to the board.

2. Cut a large circle out of tag board and divide it into pie-shaped sections. Label each section with two words that can be made into a contraction. Nail the circle to the center of the board so that it can turn easily. (Or insert a push pin through the center of the circle so that it turns.)

3. Label each clothespin with a corresponding contraction. Staple the box to the board and place the clothespins in it.

4. Make a score card and either laminate it or cover it with an acetate sheet. Staple this to the board.

Using the Board:

Students use the stop watch to time themselves as they clip the clothespins to the proper sections of the tag board wheel. They then record their scores on the score card with a grease pencil.

Make several sets of tag board sheets with corresponding clothespins so that when the students become familiar with one set of contractions, another can replace it.

This bulletin board activity can also be adjusted to practice *synonyms* (a clothespin labeled "GLAD" clipped to a section labeled "HAPPY"), *antonyms* (a clothespin labeled "GOOD" clipped to a section labeled "BAD"), and *homonyms* (a clothespin labeled "DEER" clipped to a section labeled "DEAR").

STRING ART ARITHMETIC

Purpose: Students practice their arithmetic skills while making artistic shapes with string.

Materials:

1. White paper to cover the board
2. Pushpins
3. Construction paper
4. Three cardboard boxes
5. Tag board
6. String or yarn
7. Scissors
8. Felt-tipped marker
9. One spirit master

Making the board:

1. Cover the board with white paper. Cut the words "STRING ART ARITHMETIC" out of construction paper and staple them to the top of the board.

2. Insert the pushpins into the board, evenly spaced as shown, and number them with the marker pen.

3. Staple the three boxes to the board. Fill one with string or yarn, and scissors.

16

4. Fill the second box with work sheets. To make the work sheets, divide a spirit master in half. On one half, draw lines for working out arithmetic problems. On the other half, make a copy of the bulletin board design. Include the numbers and use dots to represent the pushpins.

5. Place the code cards in the third box. Make these on pieces of tag board. With a felt-tipped marker write a series of arithmetic problems whose answers will be a series of numbers the student can use as a code to make a string art shape.

Using the Board:

A student chooses a code card and a work sheet. At his or her desk, the child figures out the problems on the lined portion of the work sheet. He or she must not write on the code card.

The student returns to the board and replaces the code card. By following his or her answers, the child loops string around each pushpin labeled with the corresponding numbers to make a shape.

Encourage students to use the other half of the work sheet to create their own shapes. They can then figure out a series of arithmetic problems that will have answers that make their shapes. The answers are written on a new code card for the rest of the class to use.

It may be helpful to have the entire class work out a shape and the appropriate problems together to introduce this activity and to familiarize the students with the concepts involved.

The code for making the butterfly shape shown is:
5, 15, 25, 35, 45, 55, 65, 74, 73, 82, 81, 71, 62, 53, 44, 43, 32, 22, 12, 3, 14, 24, 35, 36, 46, 56, 66, 77, 78, 89, 90, 80, 69, 58, 47, 48, 39, 29, 19, 8, 17, 27, 36, 65, 66, 35, 36, 26, 16, 6.

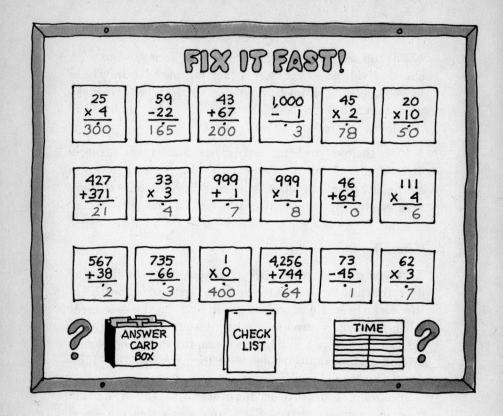

FIX IT FAST!

Purpose: Students review their knowledge of arithmetic facts and practice solving problems quickly in their heads.

Materials:

1. Construction paper
2. Tag board
3. Black and red felt-tipped markers
4. Map pins
5. Stop watch
6. Paper hole punch
7. Cardboard box
8. Acetate sheet
9. Grease pencil

Making the Board:

1. Cut the words "FIX IT FAST!" out of construction paper and staple them to the top of the board.

2. Cut the tag board into rectangles, and label them with arithmetic problems that are challenging to the students, and yet easy enough for them to solve in their heads. Write the problem in black and make up a *wrong* answer and write it in red.

3. Staple the problem cards to the board. Push a map pin into the board under each problem.

4. Cut smaller cards out of tag board and label these with the *correct* answers in black. Punch a hole in the top of each answer card so that it can hang on the map pins.

5. Staple the box to the bottom of the board and place the tag board answer cards in this box.

6. Make a check list with the correct answers and staple it to the board.

7. Make a time card and either laminate it or cover it with an acetate sheet. Staple it to the board.

Using the Board:

Students time themselves with the stop watch as they mentally correct the arithmetic mistakes and place the answer cards on the board *over* the wrong answers. They then check themselves against the check list. If all is correct, they record their time on the time card using the grease pencil.

The problems on the board can be changed weekly by a group of students.

SET THE TABLE

Purpose: Students practice measuring with the metric system and develop an awareness of the size in centimeters of familiar objects.

Materials:

1. Large piece of brightly colored paper
2. Tag board
3. Construction paper
4. Map pins
5. Felt-tipped markers
6. Crayons
7. Three cardboard boxes
8. Metric measurement rulers
9. Paper hole punch

Making the Board:

1. Cut the words "SET THE TABLE" out of construction paper and staple them to the top of the board.

2. Cover the center of the board with the brightly colored paper, scalloping the lower edge to form a "tablecloth." Allow your students to decorate the tablecloth.

3. Staple the three boxes to the board and label them "refrigerator," "cupboard," and "freezer."

4. Have each of your students choose an item of food or kitchen implement that would belong in one of these three categories. Have them make their items to size out of tag board and decorate them. Punch a hole in the top of each one.

5. Measure the items in centimeters at the widest (or longest) part and label the measurement in small numerals on the back of the item. Place the items in the proper boxes on the board.

6. Push map pins into the tablecloth and label them with numerals corresponding to those on the tag board items.

Using the Board:

Students choose an item from one of the three boxes, measure it with a metric ruler and hang it on the map pin with the corresponding numeral. The numeral on the back of the item can be used to check the student's measurement.

When the students begin to develop a feeling for metric measurement and the size of centimeters, they can place the tag board items on the board by approximating their size. The items can be constantly changed by the students to keep the activity challenging.

DANGER: SPEED ZONE!

Purpose: Students practice their multiplication facts and increase their speed in solving problems.

Materials:

1. White paper to cover the board
2. Felt-tipped marker
3. Tag board
4. Map pins
5. Two cardboard boxes
6. Construction paper
7. Paper hole punch

Making the board:

1. Cover the board with white paper. Cut the words "DANGER: SPEED ZONE!" out of construction paper and staple them to the top of the board.

2. Divide the board in half. Write the multiplication facts with which your students need the most practice on both sides of the board. Write the same facts on both sides, but write them in a different order so that the students won't copy from one another.

3. Cut the tag board into squares and write the answers to the problems on them. Punch a hole in the top of each square for hanging.

4. Staple the boxes to the bottom of the board on each side and place duplicate sets of answer cards in each box.

5. Make a check list for each side of the board and staple it to the board.

Using the Board:

Students use the board two at a time, and race with each other to correctly complete their side. They then check themselves against the check list and correct any wrong answers before they are finished. The multiplication facts can be written in both a horizontal and vertical fashion as shown.

23

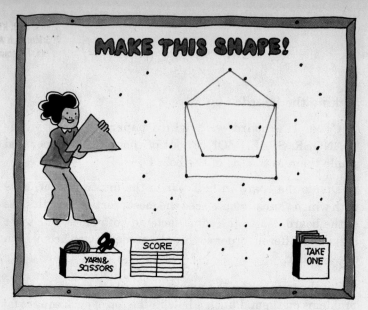

MAKE THIS SHAPE!

SAMPLE ACTIVITY CARDS

ACTIVITY CARD #1

MAKE A SQUARE

SCORE: 1 POINT

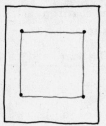

ACTIVITY CARD #2

MAKE A PENTAGON AND A SQUARE THAT INTERSECTS AT TWO POINTS

SCORE: 5 POINTS

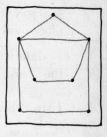

MAKE THIS SHAPE!

Purpose: Students review their knowledge of geometric shapes and concepts.

Materials:

1. Pushpins
2. Brightly colored thick yarn
3. Construction paper
4. Tag board
5. Acetate sheet
6. Two small boxes
7. Scissors
8. Felt-tipped marker
9. Grease pencil

Making the Board:

1. Cut the words "MAKE THIS SHAPE!" out of construction paper and staple them to the board.

2. Cut the tag board into cards and label them with geometric activities. (See sample activity cards.) Put the instructions on one side of the card and draw the correct shape on the other. Staple the box to the board and place the activity cards in it.

3. Make a score card out of tag board and cover it with an acetate sheet or laminate it. Staple it to the board.

4. Staple the second small box to the board and fill it with the yarn and scissors.

5. Place the pushpins in the board in a manner to correspond with the activity cards.

Using the Board:

A student chooses a card and makes the required shape by looping the yarn around the pushpins, knotting it, and cutting it off at the proper point. If the shape made is correct, the student scores the number of points indicated on the front of the card.

More points are given for more difficult activities. Terms like *intersect, symmetrical* and *asymmetrical* can be used on the more difficult activity cards, allowing the students an opportunity to practice their understanding of geometric concepts, as well as their knowledge of geometric shapes.

As the students progress the activities can become more difficult. Encourage them to add their own activity cards to the board. This can be done as a class activity.

FLOWER POWER

Purpose: Students review their knowledge of the parts of a flower and its purpose as the reproductive system of a plant.

Materials:

1. Light blue and brown paper (to cover board)
2. Construction paper
3. Tag board
4. Two cardboard boxes (one smaller than the other)
5. Map pins
6. Paper hole punch
7. Colored felt-tipped markers
8. Crayons

Making the Board:

1. Cover the top part of the board with light blue paper (sky) and the bottom with brown paper (soil).

2. Cut the words "FLOWER POWER" out of construction paper and staple them to the top of the board.

3. Outline the plant and flower parts on the blue and brown paper, including the roots, stem, leaves, sepals, petals, stamen, and pistil. Also draw and color a worm, bird, butterfly, and bee.

4. Use the tag board to make each of the plant parts. Have your students color them.

5. Place map pins on the board and punch corresponding holes in the tag board shapes so that each piece will hang properly on the board.

6. Staple the larger box to the board and place the tag board shapes in it.

7. Cut the remaining tag board into squares. Make clue cards by writing bits of information on the cards that refer to one of the tag board pieces, such as:
  "Its color attracts birds and insects to the flower." (petal)
Staple the smaller box to the board and put the clue cards into it. Make several clue cards for each tag board shape.

8. Make a check sheet for the students to use which lists the clue card information and the proper tag board shape. Staple this to the board.

Using the Board:

Students choose a clue card, decide which shape the clue refers to, and then hang the proper shape on the board over the map pins. (Some shapes may need two holes and two map pins on which to hang.) The check sheet can be used as a guide. Encourage students to help in making up the clue cards. Change the cards often to keep the board challenging.

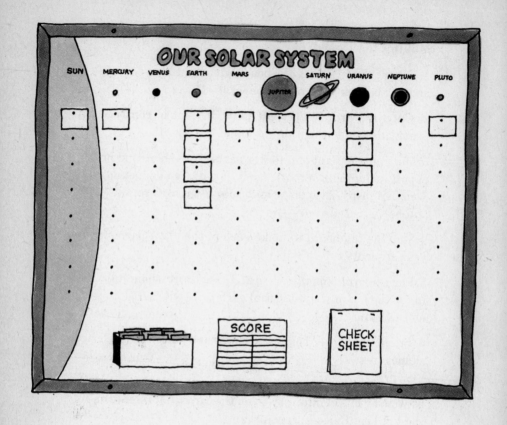

OUR SOLAR SYSTEM

Purpose: Students review their knowledge of facts about our solar system.

Materials:

1. Construction paper
2. White paper to cover the board
3. Tag board
4. Map pins
5. Paper hole punch
6. Cardboard box
7. Acetate sheet
8. Grease pencil
9. Colored felt-tipped markers
10. Crayons

Making the Board:

1. Cover the board with white paper. Draw the sun and planets on the paper across the top of the board, leaving room for the heading. Let your students decorate them.

2. Cut the words "OUR SOLAR SYSTEM" out of construction paper and staple them to the top of the board. Label the sun and planets with the markers.

3. Cut the tag board into squares and punch a hole in the top of each square. Write a fact about the sun or one of the planets on each square. Allow your students to research the facts for you. You will need about 10 facts or clue cards for each planet and for the sun. Examples of typical clue cards are as follows:

> The planet closest to the sun. (Mercury)
> The largest planet. (Jupiter)

Staple the box to the board and place the clue cards in it.

4. Push map pins into the board beneath each of the planets and the sun for the clue cards to hang on.

5. Make a score card and cover it with an acetate sheet or laminate it. Staple it to the board.

6. Use the facts on the clue cards to make a check sheet so that the students can correct themselves. Staple it to the board.

Using the Board:

Students take turns choosing clue cards, reading the facts, and hanging them in the proper place. If the card is correctly placed, the student scores a point.

The game continues until all the cards are used. The student with the most points wins. Change the clue cards when necessary to keep the game challenging.

WHO DID WHAT?

Purpose: Students review their knowledge of facts about inventors and inventions and practice writing conversational sentences.

Materials:

1. White paper to cover board
2. Small box
3. Acetate sheets
4. Grease pencils
5. Colored felt-tipped markers
6. Crayons
7. Tag board
8. Construction paper

Making the Board:

1. Cover the board with white paper. Cut the words "WHO DID WHAT?" out of construction paper and staple them to the top of the board.

2. Draw the two inventors and let your students decorate them with crayons and markers.

3. Cut two cartoon dialogue balloons out of tag board and either laminate them or cover them with acetate sheets. Staple them to the board.

4. Cut the remaining tag board into squares to make question cards. On one side of the question card, write a question or series of questions about an inventor or an invention. On the opposite side, write the answer(s). Staple the box to the board and place the question cards in it.

5. Make a score card and either laminate it or cover it with an acetate sheet. Staple it to the board.

Using the Board:

One student picks a question card and writes the question *in his or her own words* with a grease pencil in the cartoon balloon. Another student answers by writing in the other balloon with a grease pencil. If the answer is correct, the student scores a point. This is a silent bulletin board activity, for anything the students have to say to each other can be written in the balloons.

Encourage students to use the question cards as a starting point for conversations about any inventor or invention, without worrying about the score card. The research for the preparation of the question cards can be a class assignment.

The following is a list of inventors you may wish to give to your class:

James Watt, Eli Whitney, Robert Fulton, Cyrus McCormick, Gail Borden, Charles Goodyear, Thomas Edison, Carl Benz, Wilbur and Orville Wright, Alexander Graham Bell, Louis Braille.

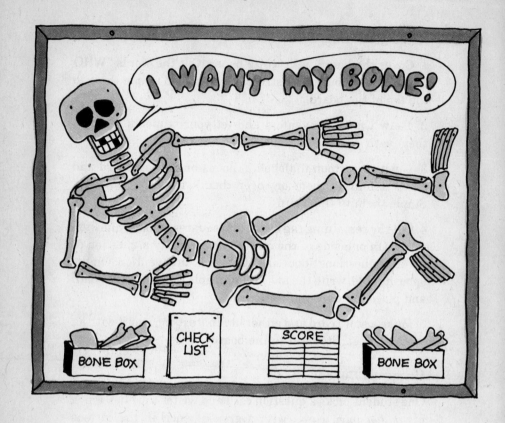

I WANT MY BONE!

Purpose: Students review their knowledge of the major bones in the body and how they connect to form the skeleton.

Materials:

1. White paper to cover the board
2. Tag board
3. Construction paper
4. Map pins
5. Two cardboard boxes
6. Acetate sheet
7. Grease pencil
8. Felt-tipped marker
9. Paper hole punch
10. Opaque projector
11. Picture of the skeleton

Making the Board:

1. Cover the board with white paper. Using the opaque projector and the picture of the skeleton, draw the skeleton on the board outlining the bones with the marker. Decide what minor bones you don't want to include, if any.

2. Draw a cartoon dialogue balloon at the top of the board. Cut the words "I WANT MY BONE" out of construction paper and staple them inside the balloon.

3. Make matching tag board bones that exactly fit over the bones on the board.

4. Place map pins in the board and punch corresponding holes in the tag board bones so that the bones can be placed over the drawing.

5. Number the tag board bones. Make a check list of the numbered bones and their names. Staple it to the board.

6. Staple two cardboard boxes to the board and place the tag board bones in these boxes.

7. Make a score card and either laminate it or cover it with an acetate sheet and staple it to the board.

Using the Board:

Students take turns choosing a tag board bone, saying its proper name and placing it in the correct place on the skeleton. If a student does all this correctly, he or she scores a point.

Students check each other by using the check list of bone names. When all the bones are placed, the student with the most points wins.

CREATURES FROM THE DEEP

Purpose: Students review their knowledge of ocean life, as well as create a mosaic design.

Materials:

1. White paper to cover the board
2. Construction paper
3. Opaque projector
4. Felt-tipped marker
5. Paste or glue
6. Photograph of an ocean scene

Making the Board:

1. Cover the board with white paper. Using the opaque projector, draw the ocean scene onto the paper. Outline all the shapes with a marker.

2. Cut the words "CREATURES FROM THE DEEP" out of construction paper and staple them to the top of the board.

3. Place construction paper in an assortment of colors and a jar of paste or glue on a small table near the board.

Using the Board:

Explain how a mosaic is made. Discuss with the class what colors each of the parts of their bulletin board mosaic should be. Label them.

Have a student demonstrate the mosaic process by tearing several pieces of construction paper and gluing them side by side on the board. Permit students to work on the mosaic in their spare time.

This bulletin board activity can be a starting point for Art History lessons as well as a study of marine life. Any subject your class is studying which lends itself to a scene can be turned into a mosaic bulletin board.

THE 50 STATES

Purpose: Students review their knowledge of the names, locations, and abbreviations of the fifty states in the United States.

Materials:

1. White paper to cover the board
2. Opaque projector
3. Map of the U.S.
4. Construction paper
5. Tag board
6. Map pins
7. Felt-tipped marker
8. Paper hole punch
9. Cardboard box
10. Stop watch

Making the board:

1. Cover the board with white paper and project the map of the U.S. onto it. Let the students outline the map and draw in the state boundaries with a marker. Place a map pin in the center of each state.

2. Cut the words "THE 50 STATES" out of construction paper and staple them to the top of the board.

3. Cut squares out of tag board and label them with the state abbreviations. Punch a hole in the top of each square. Staple the box to the board and put the tag board squares in it.

4. On construction paper, write a list of the state names and their postal abbreviations. Staple this to the board.

Using the Board:

Students pick the labels out of the box and hang them on the map pins in the appropriate states, using, if needed, the list of state names and abbreviations for reference. Students can use a stop watch to time themselves.

GEORGE AND ABE

Purpose: Students review their knowledge of American history facts and practice writing dialogue.

Materials:

1. White paper to cover the board
2. Construction paper
3. Tag board
4. Small box
5. Colored felt-tipped markers.
6. Acetate sheets
7. Opaque projector
8. Grease pencils
9. Crayons
10. Pictures of Abraham Lincoln and George Washington

Making the Board:

1. Cover the board with white paper. Using the opaque projector and the pictures of Abe and George, draw the two presidents on the paper. Allow your students to color them with crayons and markers.

2. Cut two cartoon balloons out of tag board and either laminate them or cover them with acetate sheets. Staple them to the board.

3. Cut the remaining tag board into rectangles for question cards. Label each card with a question about American history such as:

    When was the Declaration of Independence signed?
    Who were two important generals who fought in the
    Civil War?
Put the answers to the questions on the reverse side of the card. Staple the box to the board and place the cards in it.

4. Make a score card and either laminate it or cover it with an acetate sheet. Staple it to the board.

Using the Board:

One student picks a question card and, using a grease pencil, writes the question *in his or her own words* in one cartoon balloon. Another student answers the question by writing in the other balloon. If the student has the correct answer, he or she scores a point. This is a silent bulletin board activity, for anything the students have to say to each other can be written in the balloons.

    Encourage students to use the question cards as a starting point for conversations about anything referring to American history (without worrying about the score card). New question cards can be added by the students as a class activity.

IT'S MY OPINION

Purpose: Students consider current events problems and express their opinions about them.

Materials:

1. White paper to cover board
2. Construction paper
3. Colored felt-tipped markers
4. Crayons
5. Tag board
6. Acetate sheets
7. Cardboard box
8. Grease pencils

Making the Board:

1. Cover the board with white paper. Draw the two figures on the board and let your students decorate the board with markers and crayons. Cut the words "IT'S MY OPINION"

out of construction paper and staple them to the top of the board.

2. Cut two cartoon dialogue balloons and a rectangle out of tag board and either laminate them or cover them with acetate sheets. Staple the balloons to the board. Staple the rectangle under the heading "INTERVIEWEE" on the back of the "chair."

3. Cut squares from the remaining tag board. Have your students each make up several cards to contribute to the board. Each card should be made up of a series of questions concerning a current events subject, such as a reporter might ask a politician in a press conference. Staple the box to the board and place the interview cards in the box.

4. Have your students aid you in making up a list of appropriate interviewees. These should be names of prominent political figures. List the names on an "INTERVIEWEE" sheet and staple it to the board.

Using the Board:

This is a silent activity for everything the students need to say to one another can be written in the balloons. One student is the reporter and chooses an interview card from which he writes questions for the interviewee. The other student, who is the interviewee, can either choose to be him- or herself and write his or her own name on the back of the chair, or can choose a name from the list of interviewees and write this name on the chair.

Students choosing to be themselves give their own opinions. Students choosing to be someone else must do their best to express the opinions of that political figure.

This bulletin board activity can be preceeded by class discussion about the list of interviewees and what their opinions are, with newspaper articles brought in as supporting evidence. Also, to familiarize the students with the idea of interviewing, some role-playing can be done.

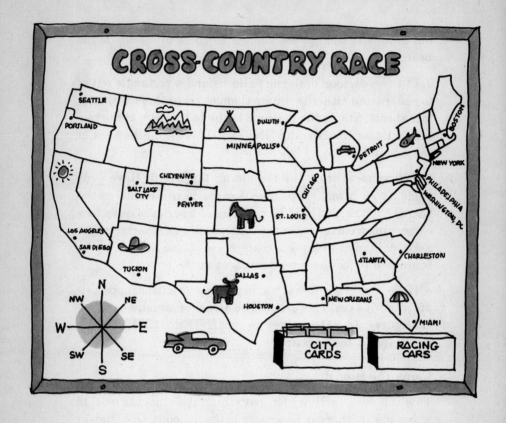

CROSS-COUNTRY RACE

Purpose: Students increase their awareness of the locations of major cities in the United States and practice reading directions.

Materials:

1. White paper to cover the board
2. Construction paper
3. Tag board
4. Two cardboard boxes
5. Pushpins
6. Colored felt-tipped markers
7. Opaque projector
8. Map of the U.S.

Making the Board:

1. Cover the board with white paper. Cut the words "CROSS-COUNTRY RACE" out of construction paper and staple them to the top of the board.

2. Using the opaque projector and the map of the U.S., draw the United States (excluding Alaska and Hawaii) on the paper. Label about 20 to 25 major cities. Allow the students to decorate the map with markers or crayons, illustrating the various products which typify each section of the country.

3. Draw a compass rose on the board, labeling the directions.

4. Cut tag board into squares to make city cards. Write humorous instructions on these cards, such as:
   Your Aunt's dog just had 16 puppies. Travel to *Dallas,*
   Texas to pick one out.
Staple the box to the board and place the cards in it. Make several city cards for each city.

5. Make small tag board race cars and place them in the other box with pushpins. Staple this box to the board.

Using the Board:

Students choose a car and a pushpin and place their cars in New York City. They take turns choosing city cards and traveling to the city named on the card. After moving their race car to the designated city, they must state which direction they just traveled.

Students use the compass rose to check each other. If a wrong direction is given, the student loses a turn.

The object of the game is to race across the country to the west coast and back again to the east coast to win. Reaching any city in a coastal state is regarded as reaching the coast.

Students can take an active part in preparing this board by making up the city cards and making their own race cars. When the class has become familiar with the major cities in the U.S., label other cities and make up new city cards to correspond to them.

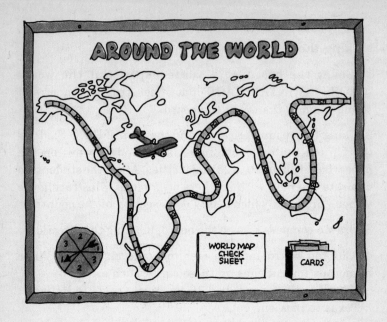

AROUND THE WORLD

Purpose: Students review their knowledge of the world's continents, countries, and oceans.

Materials:

1. White paper to cover the board
2. Opaque projector
3. Map of the world
4. Colored felt-tipped markers
5. Crayons
6. Pushpins
7. Tag board
8. Small cardboard box
9. Construction paper
10. Gold foil stars

Making the Board:

1. Cover the board with white paper. Use the world map and opaque projector to copy the map onto the board. Allow the students to decorate the map with crayons and felt-tipped markers.

2. Cut the words "AROUND THE WORLD" out of construction paper and staple them to the top of the board.

3. Draw a trail over the continents from one side of the board to the other. Glue gold stars at different points along the trail.

4. Make a spinner out of tag board. Attach a construction paper arrow to the center of the spinner with a brass paper fastener, so that the arrow can spin when flicked with a finger. Staple spinner to the board.

5. Make a world map check sheet labeled with continents, oceans, and countries and staple it to the board.

6. Cut the remaining tag board into star cards. Label some of the cards with questions such as:
  What is the continent that is also a country? (Australia)
  What are four oceans in the world? (Atlantic, Pacific, Indian, and Arctic)
Label some of these cards with instructions such as:
  Go to Detroit, Michigan and work in an automobile factory.
  Go to China and work in a rice field.

Using the Board:

Students use pushpins as markers and start at one end of the trail. Each student spins and moves his or her marker the appropriate number of spaces.

If the student lands on a gold star, he or she chooses a star card and must fulfill its command. If the star card is a question, the other students use the check sheet to check the answer. If the star card is an instruction, the student must find the proper location on the map and place his or her finger there until it is again his or her turn. In this manner, the students become familiar with facts about the world and practice locating countries on the map. If a student cannot fulfill the command of a star card, he or she loses a turn.

The first student to go around the world by reaching the end of the trail, wins the game. Permit students to add their own star cards to the board. This can be done as a class project, with each student responsible for making one question and one instruction star card.

NOTES

NOTES